STAR WARS
THE LAST JEDI
THE OFFICIAL COLLECTOR'S EDITION

TITAN EDITORIAL
Editor Jonathan Wilkins
Senior Executive Editor Divinia Fleary
Copy Editor Simon Hugo
Contributing Editor Nick Jones
Editorial Assistant Jake Devine
Senior Production Controller Jackie Flook
Production Supervisor Maria Pearson
Production Controller Peter James
Art Director Oz Browne
Senior Sales Manager Steve Tothill
Circulation Assistant Frankie Hallam

Subscriptions Executive Tony Ho
Direct Sales & Marketing Manager
Ricky Claydon
Brand Manager, Marketing Lucy Ripper
Commercial Manager Michelle Fairlamb
Advertising Assitant Tom Miller
US Advertising Manager Jeni Smith
Publishing Manager Darryl Tothill
Publishing Director Chris Teather
Operations Director Leigh Baulch
Executive Director Vivian Cheung
Publisher Nick Landau

DISTRIBUTION
U.S. Newsstand: Total Publisher Services, Inc.
John Dziewiatkowski, 630-851-7683
U.S. Distribution: Ingrams Periodicals, Curtis
Circulation Company
U.K. Newsstand: Marketforce, 0203 787 9199
U.S./U.K. Direct Sales Market: Diamond
Comic Distributors
For more info on advertising contact
adinfo@titanemail.com

Printed in the US by Quad.

Contents © 2017 Lucasfilm Ltd. & TM.
All Rights Reserved

Star Wars: The Last Jedi The Official Collector's Edition is published by Titan Magazines, a division of Titan Publishing Group Limited, 144 Southwark Street, London SE1 0UP

For sale in the U.S., Canada, U.K., and Eire

ISBN: 9781785862113
Titan Authorized User. TMN 13428

DISNEY PUBLISHING WORLDWIDE GLOBAL
MAGAZINES, COMICS AND PARTWORKS
Publisher Lynn Waggoner
Editorial Director Bianca Coletti
Director, Comics Guido Frazzini
Executive Editor, New IP Stefano Ambrosio
Executive Editor, Franchise Carlotta Quattrocolo

Senior Manager, Editorial Development
Camilla Vedove
Senior Editor Behnoosh Khalili
Senior Editor Julie Dorris
Senior Designer Enrico Soave
VP, Global Art Ken Shue
Creative Director Roberto Santillo

Creative Manager Marco Ghiglione
Creative Manager Manny Mederos
Computer Art Designer Stefano Attardi
Director Olivia Ciancarelli
Senior Manager, Franchise Mariantonietta Galla
Editorial Manager Virpi Korhonen
Text Alessandro Ferrari

Graphic Design n co-d S.r.l. – Milano
Pre=Press co-d S.r.l. – Milano, Lito milano srl

LUCASFILM EDITORIAL
Senior Editor Brett Rector
Image Archives Newell Todd, Bryce Pinkos,
Gabrielle Levenson, Erik Sanchez

Art Director Troy Alders
Story Group Leland Chee,
Pablo Hidlago, Matt Martin
Creative Director Michael Siglain
Special Thanks: Lynne Hale,
Chris Argyropoulos, Brian Miller,
Steve Newman, Phil Szostak

Art by Kevin Jenkins

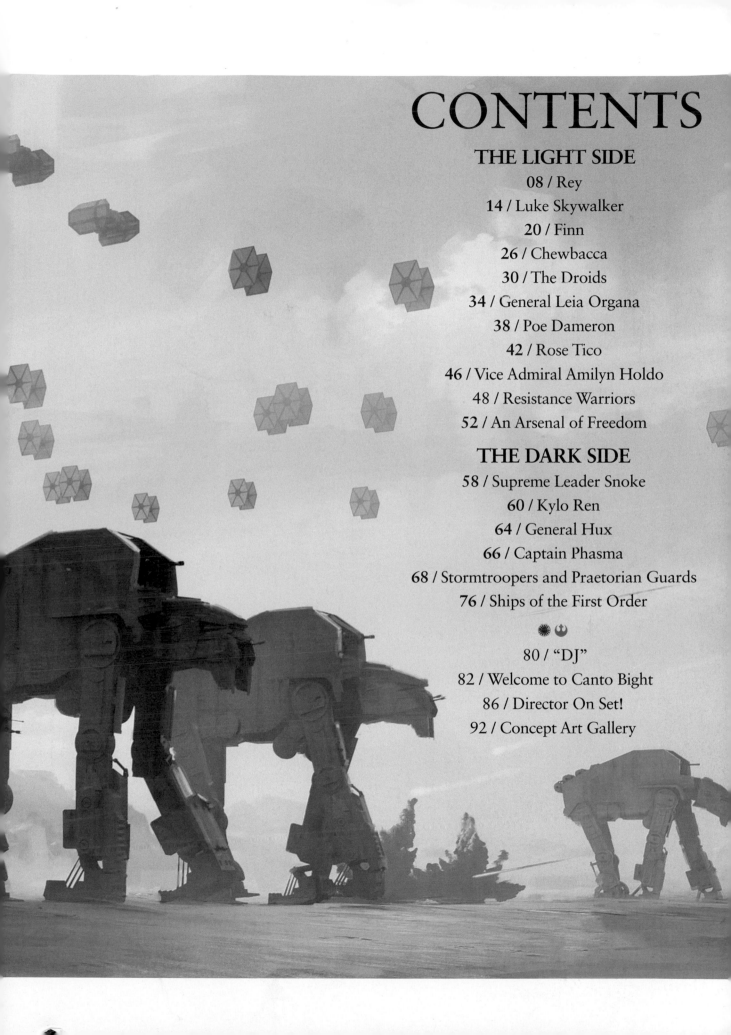

CONTENTS

THE LIGHT SIDE

THE DARK SIDE

THE LIGHT SIDE

SIDE

As the heroes of the Resistance flee the wrath of the
First Order, Rey encounters the mysterious Luke Skywalker.

REY
MAY THE FORCE BE WITH HER

The Force has awakened in Rey. But for her powers to be put at the service of the Resistance, she needs guidance.

Abandoned by her parents as a child, Rey lived alone on the desert planet of Jakku, waiting—hoping—for her family's eventual return. To survive in this harsh, unforgiving environment, she became a scavenger and a fighter, but each night she gazed up at the stars, longing for something more.

Rey's life radically changed when she encountered Finn, a fugitive stormtrooper on the run from the First Order, and BB-8, an astromech droid belonging to Resistance fighter Poe Dameron. Forming an alliance, Rey, Finn, and BB-8 fled an attack by the nefarious First Order, blasting away from Jakku aboard a starship they stole from a junkyard: the *Millennium Falcon*. Linking up with the ship's rightful owners, Han Solo and Chewbacca—former heroes of the Rebel Alliance against the Empire who had returned to a life of smuggling, they joined the Resistance against the First Order.

On the planet Takodana, Rey learned about the Force, a mystical, invisible energy that surrounds and penetrates all living things, binding the galaxy together. To her surprise, she discovered she had a strong connection to the Force, so strong that, on Starkiller Base —an entire planet converted into a superweapon by the First Order—she was able to hold her own against the powerful Kylo Ren in a lightsaber duel… and even best him.

Even so, Rey's nascent abilities could easily lead her to the dark side of the Force. Realizing that she needed the wisdom of a Jedi Master to guide her along the right path, Rey sought out the legendary Luke Skywalker. She found him on an island on the remote world of Ahch-To—a place familiar to her from visions she experienced whilst still on Jakku—but when she hands Luke his old lightsaber,

the weapon built by his father Anakin Skywalker, alias Darth Vader, he rejects it. Moreover, when she asks him to help her and the Resistance, by rejoining their ranks and opposing the First Order, he refuses. As far as Luke is concerned, the Jedi must end.

As stubborn as she is tenacious, Rey doesn't relent—the stakes are far too high for her to give in now. Finally, with a little assistance from Luke's old astromech droid, R2-D2, she persuades the old master to teach her the ways of the Force.

Initially, Luke merely wants her to understand his reasons and then leave, but Rey proves to be of a different order from anyone else he has ever trained. Her mysterious bond to the dark side and to Kylo Ren is something Skywalker has never seen before —a, powerful and dangerous connection. But it's only through that bond that Rey will be able to understand who she really is. ☸

2 /

3 /

4 /

1 / The mysterious Rey.
(See previous page)

2 / Lightsaber ignited!
Will Rey become a Jedi?

3 / Rey recovers from
seeing an intense
image in the Force.

4 / In training with her
trusty staff on Ahch-To.

5 / Rey refuses to
be defeated by
Luke's apathy.
(See opposite page)

6 / Rey takes the
gunning station of the
Millennium Falcon as
the First Order
closes in!

LUKE SKYWALKER

BEYOND THE LAST HOPE

Choosing to go into exile after his dream of a new training school turns into a nightmare, Luke looks to be the last Jedi. Is this really the end of the order that once protected the galaxy?

For what seemed like an eternity to him, Luke Skywalker lived on the remote desert world of Tatooine with his Aunt Beru and Uncle Owen. A restless farm boy, Luke dreamed of a life of adventure—of being able to attend the Imperial Academy and becoming an ace pilot.

Luke had always been told by his uncle that his father, Anakin Skywalker, had been a navigator aboard a spice freighter. But the younger Skywalker's life changed forever when he learned that not only was Anakin in fact a Jedi Knight who fought in the Clone Wars, but also that he subsequently became Darth Vader, the Emperor's most feared and powerful emissary, and a champion of the dark side of the Force.

Events repeatedly brought Luke into conflict with his father. An encounter at Cloud City, high above Bespin, had Luke wielding Anakin's own lightsaber against him, but he ultimately lost it—along with his right hand. Later, at the climax of another epic duel, this time on a reconstituted Death Star, Luke resisted the lure of the dark side only to come under attack by the watching Emperor. Stricken at Luke's plight, Darth Vader repented, his compassion for his son ultimately defeating the Emperor—albeit at the cost of Vader's life—and saving the galaxy, restoring peace and freedom.

For many years thereafter, Luke chose not to take on an apprentice, until he came to realize just how powerful his nephew was. Ben Solo, the son of Han Solo and Luke's sister, Leia Organa, had the Skywalker blood flowing through his veins, and therefore had a natural affinity with the Force. Luke took Ben and a group of students and established a training temple, hoping to revive the defunct Jedi Order. But the darkness rising in Ben was uncontrollable, and led the young apprentice to commit a terrible act of betrayal. Ben destroyed the temple and killed his fellow students.

The balance between the light and the dark was shattered. Holding himself responsible for the tragedy, Luke attempted to bury the past—and the Jedi Order along with it—by vanishing. He headed for the remote world of Ahch-To, far from his sister Leia, who desperately needed him to join the fight against the First Order.

Electing to live a simple life, Luke follows a strict routine, from harvesting everything he needs from the island to taking shelter inside an ancient hut. It is a life of quiet solitude away from galactic conflict—until the fateful day the *Millennium Falcon* appeared on the horizon, and the past came calling in the form of his father's long lost lightsaber, offered to him by a young, Force-sensitive woman. ☻

1 / Luke Skywalker,
hero of the Rebellion
and lost Jedi. (See
previous page)

2 / Rey attempts
to persuade the
last Jedi to return.
(See opposite page)

3 / Luke Skywalker
is reunited with a
piece of his past.

4 / Inside a mysterious
tree, Luke consults
with ancient Jedi texts.

5 /

6 /

5 / Jedi Master Luke
Skywalker ponders
the mysteries of Rey.

6 / Luke Skywalker,
a Jedi in exile.

FINN
A MAN ON A MISSION

Everyone thinks he's a hero, but former stormtrooper Finn sure doesn't feel like one. The only thing he cares about is finding Rey and keeping her safe.

Abducted from his home planet, a young boy given the serial number FN-2187 was trained to become a First Order stormtrooper. Required to follow orders without question, he was sent into battle under the leadership of Captain Phasma, but he was unable to obey her directive.

When the opportunity arose to help captured Resistance pilot Poe Dameron escape from a First Order Star Destroyer, FN-2187 seized it. The pair hijacked a Special Forces TIE fighter and high-tailed it out of the ship. As they escaped, Dameron renamed his rescuer Finn. However, their daring getaway went awry when they were shot down and crash-landed back on Jakku.

Believing Poe was killed in the crash, Finn wandered the desert planet, eventually encountering Rey, a tough, young woman with a kind heart. Though Finn's only desire was to get as far away from the First Order as possible, when Rey was captured by the Order's Kylo Ren, Finn resolved to fight.

Aboard the *Millennium Falcon*, Finn journeyed to Starkiller Base, the First Order's superweapon. There, he tried to protect Rey from Ren, but was seriously injured during a lightsaber duel. Unconscious, Finn was brought aboard the *Falcon,* and he is later transferred to the Resistance flagship *Raddus*, where doctors place him in an emergency bacta suit to recover.

When Finn comes to, he is under the false impression that he is still on Starkiller Base. He is unaware that Rey has traveled to Ahch-To to train to become a Jedi, or that the Resistance fleet is being pursued across the galaxy by the First Order, which is on the verge of wiping them out. He's equally surprised to learn that everyone in the Resistance has heard his story: how he absconded from the First Order—the first time any stormtrooper has been known to do so—and helped destroy Starkiller Base. Not surprisingly, those in the Resistance believe he is a hero.

For his part, Finn isn't so sure. His only concern is in finding Rey and keeping her safe. As he attempts to leave the *Raddus*, he runs into maintenance worker Rose Tico. Together the pair devise a daring plan to help the Resistance fleet escape the First Order.

Once again, Finn is going to risk his life for the right cause—something that surely only a hero would do? ☻

JOHN BOYEGA

FINN

1 / Finn, back on his feet and ready for adventure! (See previous page)

2 / Showdown with Captain Phasma!

3 / Finn and BB-8 have struck up a friendship after a difficult start.

4 / Still recovering from wounds inflicted by Kylo Ren, Finn is awakened when the Resistance comes under attack. (See opposite page)

2 /

3 /

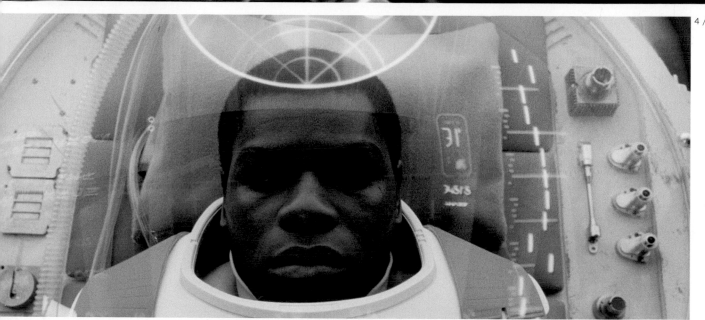

5 /

6 /

5 / Piloting a ski
speeder as the
Resistance makes
a stand!

6 / Finn and the
Resistance pilots race
toward the First Order
forces.

CHEWBACCA
THE HEART OF A WARRIOR

With Han Solo gone, the first mate of the *Millennium Falcon* is missing a captain—someone he can both depend on and take care of.

A wise and seasoned operator—despite initial appearances to the contrary—the Wookiee Chewbacca has fought and survived many battles. During the Clone Wars, in a time before the Empire asserted its dark dominion over the galaxy, Chewbacca served as a combat engineer on his home planet of Kashyyyk, fighting alongside Jedi Master Yoda and the Grand Army of the Republic against the unrelenting forces of the Separatists' battle droids.

Later, together with inveterate rogue Han Solo, he became a smuggler and a pirate. As the first mate and the captain of the *Millennium Falcon*—a heavily modified Corellian freighter—Chewie and Han traversed the galaxy trading stolen cargo in the service of assorted interplanetary crime lords, among them the repulsive and dangerous Jabba the Hutt.

It is during this time that Chewie, along with Han, encounterd a young farm boy named Luke Skywalker on the desert planet Tatooine. Along with the reclusive Jedi Master Obi-Wan Kenobi, the pair helped Luke rescue Princess Leia Organa of Alderaan from the clutches of the Imperials. Liberating her from deep within a monstrous, moon-sized weapon known as the Death Star, these unlikely compatriots subsequently assisted the Rebel Alliance in destroying the battle station. Han and Chewbacca later played a key role in taking down the Empire's more powerful second Death Star.

Some years later, when the *Millennium Falcon* was stolen, Chewie and Han searched the galaxy for their missing ship, scouring every system in an effort to locate their vessel. When they finally tracked it down, they were both are surprised to find it piloted by Rey, a woman who recently had fled the remote desert world Jakku. Agreeing to take Rey, her ally Finn, and their droid BB-8 to find the Resistance and General Organa, Chewbacca and Han wound up getting sucked into the conflict between the Resistance and the First Order. During a mission to the Starkiller Base to destroy the enemy's superweapon, Chewie lost his best friend when Han was killed at the hands of his estranged son, Kylo Ren.

For the first time in his life, the Wookiee found himself alone inside the cockpit of the *Millennium Falcon*. But his enforced solitude wasn't to last. Though Han was gone, there was still someone Chewie could help and protect—someone with an incredible talent for piloting; an individual to whom Han himself once offered a job: Rey.

Once again a first mate and copilot—roles he prefers—Chewbacca agreed to let the young scavenger fly the legendary spacecraft. Following a map, they went to the distant planet Ahch-To, where they found the self-exiled Luke Skywalker. While Rey tries to persuade Luke to teach her the ways of the Force, Chewie sticks close to the *Falcon*, waiting to see what transpires. ☻

2 /

3 /

4 /

1 / The mighty
Chewbacca roars
into action! (See
previous page)

2 / Chewie and Rey
take control of the
Millennium Falcon.

3 / A cute passenger
joins Chewbacca in
the *Falcon's* cockpit.

4 / The *Millennium
Falcon* in the heat
of battle.

ᚹᚷᚱᛃᛟᚾᛏ ᛏᚷᛗᚾᛏᚷᚾᛏ ᛏᚷᚾᛏ ᛏᛁᛟᛟᚾ ᚷᛗᛗᛁ ᚷᛏᛏᛁ

DROIDS
A FORCE TO BE RECKONED WITH

More than merely machines providing technical support and assistance, these droids have proved to be an essential part of the Resistance.

BB-8

An unassuming spherical astromech droid, BB-8 has a particular aptitude for adventure. Prior to the destruction of Starkiller Base, BB-8 joined Poe Dameron on his mission to Jakku to retrieve information vital to the whereabouts of Luke Skywalker. When the droid and Poe were forced to separate, BB-8 was entrusted with the data. Employing all his ingenuity he managed to roll away from the stormtroopers searching for him and persuaded a young woman, Rey, to help him get off the planet and back to the Resistance.

After Rey leaves for Ahch-To with R2-D2 and Chewbacca, BB-8 aids Poe Dameron in the fight against the First Order Dreadnought during the evacuation of D'Qar. Ready and willing to risk everything for the Resistance, he's determined to accompany Finn and Rose on their sabotage mission aboard the enemy's flagship. He may not have been terribly enamored of Finn at first, but BB-8 now completely trusts the former stormtrooper.

R2-D2

Long before the demise of the Galactic Republic and the rise of the Empire, R2 was already a firmly established hero. Among his many feats of courage, he repaired the Naboo Royal Starship during an invasion, helping save Queen Amidala, the future mother of Luke and Leia.

When the Empire achieved dominance over the galaxy, R2 was serving Alderaan's royal family. Pursued by Darth Vader, Leia sent the droid on a desperate mission to Tatooine, where he met Luke. Along with Luke and protocol droid C-3PO, R2 played a vital role in the events that led to the end of the Empire and a return to galactic peace.

For years thereafter, the little droid and his master Luke stuck together—until Kylo Ren destroyed everything that Luke was trying to build. When the devastated Jedi went into self-imposed exile, R2 put himself into stand-by mode, only reactivating when the other portion of the map to Luke's location was revealed. Standing by Rey's side, R2 voyaged aboard the *Millennium Falcon* to Ahch-To, where he eagerly awaits a reunion with his master.

C-3PO

As a protocol droid, C-3PO is programmed to translate alien and cyborg languages or provide valuable information about customs and etiquette—not especially useful during, say, an evacuation or escape. Nonetheless, C-3PO—who's been with R2 since the beginning—does his best to help General Leia and the Resistance leaders find a way to move the fleet out of reach of the First Order. ☻

2 /

3 /

1 / Resistance heroes C-3PO, R2-D2, and BB-8.
(See previous page)

2 / BB-8 inside Poe's X-wing making repairs
during a battle against the First Order.

3 / R2 aboard the *Millennium Falcon*.

4 / C-3PO joins the Resistance's stand on Crait.
(See opposite page)

4 /

LEIA
LIGHTING THE WAY

In their most desperate hour, the members of the Resistance look to the princess who once defeated an Empire: Leia Organa.

The daughter of Senator Padmé Amidala and Jedi Knight Anakin Skywalker, as a baby Leia was adopted by the Royal Family of the planet Alderaan. Years later, when she found herself at the mercy of the notorious Darth Vader—her father's new identity—neither of them recognized the other.

However, the Skywalker blood runs in her veins, and though Leia has never been trained as a Jedi, the Force is strong with her. Rescued by Luke Skywalker, Han Solo, and Chewbacca from captivity aboard the Death Star, Princess Leia brought the plans for the Imperial superweapon to her fellow rebels on Yavin 4. A review of the Death Star's technical readout revealed a flaw that the rebels exploited to great success, destroying the battlestation.

Thereafter, elevated to the position of one of the most influential leaders in the Alliance, Leia was also part of the team that played a crucial role in the destruction of the second Death Star, and the end of the Empire.

Years later, Leia was the first to warn the senate about the danger posed by the First Order's activities. When her entreaties to the senators to put a stop to Snoke's arms race fell on deaf ears, Leia formed the Resistance in order to oppose the First Order.

General Organa knows that the Resistance is the galaxy's only hope of restoring peace and freedom, but in order for the movement to survive, a new generation of heroes must take her place. Preparing them for that task is Leia's paramount duty. ☻

2 /

3 /

1 / Respected leader
General Leia Organa.
(See previous page)

2 / General Organa
takes command of
the *Raddus* as she
attempts to lead
the Resistance out
of danger.

3 / Through connection
of Force and blood,
Leia can sense the dark
presence of her son
leading an attack on
the Resistance fleet.

4 / The weight of
responsibilty for the
fleet weighs heavy
on the general. (See
opposite page)

POE DAMERON
THE FUTURE IN HIS HANDS

Commander Poe Dameron is the best pilot in the Resistance—but in its darkest hour, he must become far more than that.

General Organa has always trusted Poe Dameron. Mission after mission Leia has heaped greater and greater responsibility on his shoulders. Of all the Resistance's operatives, it is Poe she entrusts with the most dangerous assignments, notably when she sent him to Jakku to retrieve the map to Luke Skywalker's location.

Aboard his distinctive black X-wing, Poe led a squadron of Resistance starfighters against the First Order, first on planet Takodana, then on Starkiller Base.

His blasts started a chain reaction that ultimately led to the destruction of the ice planet.

When the First Order fleet intercepts the Resistance in the middle of the evacuation of D'Qar, Poe doesn't hesitate: following his instincts, he approaches the enemy's Dreadnought alone, aboard his light fighter, and takes out all its cannons before they realize he's merely a decoy. It's thanks to him that the bombers can start their attack in order to buy time for the evacuation to be completed.

However, Poe also has a reckless side. When General Organa orders him to disengage, Poe switches off the comm, hoping that the bombers will take down the Dreadnought. Which they do—but at a high cost… almost too high.

For his flagrant disregard of a direct order, Leia demotes him. She knows that Poe Dameron represents the future of the Resistance, but in order for him to become one of its more important members, he has to learn a vital lesson: that he cannot solve everything by jumping in his X-wing and blowing stuff up. He must learn patience and strategy; he must learn to think like a leader. ☻

2 /

4 /

1 / Poe Dameron: Hero of the Resistance. (See previous page)

2 / Poe contemplates the future of the Resistance, as dark forces gather.

3 / Leading members of the Resistance in an act of defiance against Vice Admiral Holdo.

4 / Always on the move! Dameron races into action. (See opposite page)

3 /

ROSE TICO
WORKING FOR THE GOOD GUYS

Like her sister Paige, Rose Tico has harbored a simmering hatred for the First Order ever since she was a child. Now she finally has the chance to fight back.

Raised by their parents Hue and Thanya in the Otomok system, Rose Tico and her older sister Paige grew up in the peaceful mining colony of Hays Minor. The girls dreamed of leaving their home and traveling the galaxy, of experiencing its myriad marvels...until the First Order arrived and crushed those dreams.

Unbeknownst to the Galactic Republic, the nefarious military organization began razing the cities of Otomok to test their armaments. They abducted the planet's children for recruitment purposes and left the survivors nothing to live for—except perhaps their burning hatred of the First Order.

Wearing twin medallions adorned with the symbol of the Otomok system, Paige and Rose joined the Resistance cause—the former serving as a ventral gunner aboard a bomber, the latter as a member of the support crew. A talented mechanic, Rose developed a system that makes the Resistance's spacecraft harder for enemy sensors to detect. After the evacuation of D'Qar, she guards the *Raddus'* escape pods from anyone who tries to flee.

Even before they meet him, the Tico sisters know of Finn's story. To them, his actions proved that he is a real hero—one who knew right from wrong, and who didn't simply run away when he had the chance.

When they realize the First Order has the ability to track the Resistance fleet through hyperspace, Finn and Rose devise a plan to sneak aboard the enemy's flagship and disable the tracker. In order to accomplish this, they need a codebreaker. The only place they can locate one is the casino city of Canto Bight on Cantonica: a dangerous planet populated by war profiteers and criminals... ☸

2 /

3 /

1 / Rose Tico of
the Resistance.
(See previous page)

2 / Rose and Finn
team up on a mission
for the Resistance.

3 / Finn meets an
initially less-than-
friendly Rose!

4 / Rose confronts
Finn in the casino
city Canto Bight.

5 / Rose embarks on
a life or death mission.
(See opposite page)

4 /

5 /

AMILYN HOLDO

THE VICE ADMIRAL

A member of the Resistance and a longstanding friend of General Organa, Vice Admiral Holdo takes command at a critical time for the Resistance.

With her striking dyed hair and glamorous attire, Vice Admiral Amilyn Holdo doesn't look like a typical high-ranking officer. However, her military experience dates back to her time serving the Rebel Alliance in the early days of the Galactic Civil War.

Born on the planet Gatalenta, as a teenager Amilyn Holdo joined a political organization called the Apprentice Legislature, on Coruscant. During her time there, she met Princess Leia Organa of Alderaan and the two became friends, spending a great deal of time together attending senatorial sessions and routine pathfinding training on various worlds. Whilst on one such trip, Holdo learned of her friend's involvement with the Rebellion against the Galactic Empire. Soon after, Holdo helped Organa navigate safe passage to the Paucris system so that the princess could warn the rebel fleet that the Empire was poised to attack.

Later, after the Rebellion formally became the Alliance to Restore the Republic, and after a long fight to topple the evil dictator Palpatine during the subsequent Galactic Civil War, the Empire was finally defeated.

The Alliance rebranded itself as the New Republic. But out of the ashes of the Imperial machine came a remnant reorganized into the First Order. Organa created the Resistance to oppose the First Order, with Holdo joining the cause some years later as a Vice Admiral.

When General Organa is injured as the Resistance flees the First Order, Holdo assumes command. However, while she is more than capable for the role, a number of Resistance members, chiefly Poe Dameron, bristle under her command, and are highly suspicious of her evasive manner. ☮

ᚃᛁᚁᚃᛁᚉᚆᚃᛁᚅ ᚑᚄ ᚇᛁᛂᚃᛁ ᚄᚆᚉᛂᚃᛇ ᚑᛂᛂᚃᛇ

RESISTANCE
HIGH COMMAND
FIGHTING ON THE RUN

When Leia first formed the Resistance, many heeded her call. These courageous individuals hail from an array of backgrounds—from the Rebel Alliance, from independent defense forces, and from the New Republic.

COMMANDER D'ACY

In charge of the *Raddus'* bridge crew, and personally recruited by General Leia Organa herself, Larma D'Acy hails from the Warlentta system—a region which maintained its independence after the end of the Empire and refused to join the New Republic. Her family is responsible for protecting the sovereign space of their homeworld and welcomes her decision to join the Resistance.

3 /

LIEUTENANT CONNIX

Kaydel Connix serves as an operations controller on D'Qar. During the attack on Starkiller Base, her outstanding efforts to coordinate communications with Poe Dameron's squadron marked her out from the crowd. Promoted to lieutenant, she successfully leads the planet evacuation. Once the base is fully evacuated, Connix joins the *Raddus'* crew under the command of Admiral Ackbar and supreme commander General Organa.

1 / An emergency briefing aboard the *Raddus*.(See previous page)

2 / Resistance bridge Commander Larma D'Acy. (See previous page)

3 / Lieutenant Kaydel Connix.

4 / The Resistance face the wrath of the First Order!

4 /

5 / Admiral Ackbar
takes command
aboard the *Raddus*.

V-4X-D SKI
SPEEDER

Obsolete vehicles which
predate even the Rebellion
era, these ultra-light, low
altitude crafts, also known
as skim speeders, are used
during the Resistance's
defence on Crait.

AN ARSENAL
OF FREEDOM

The Resistance's efforts against the First Order's impressive
fleet may seem to be hopeless, but they have a few ships that
might just hold back their foe's attack.

T-70 X-WING

Perhaps the most easily identifiable starfighter in the Resistance's fleet, and the most advanced after the updated T-85s were understood to have all been destroyed in the Starkiller Base's attack on the Hosnian system.

RZ-2 A-WING INTERCEPTOR

Fast and maneuverable, the A-wing served the Rebel Alliance in the Galactic Civil War, and has been modified with refined cannon mountings, streamlining, and improvements to the jammers, making the craft far harder for enemies to target.

MILLENNIUM FALCON

Modified by its former owner, the late Han Solo, and his first mate, Chewbacca, into a speedier vessel, the *Falcon* is still a formidable ship despite its considerable age.

MG-100
STARFORTRESS

A bomber that was first used during the Galactic Civil War, this craft saw active service in peacetime when it was modified to perform cargo drops, wildfire suppression, and deploy explosives for mining.

ꟿꟿꟿ ꟿꟿꟿꟿꟿ ꟿꟿꟿꟿꟿ

THE DARK SIDE

Sinister and malevolent, the evil forces of Supreme
Leader Snoke, led by Kylo Ren, are poised to crush
the Resistance...

ᚲᚢᚨᚱᚢ ᚾᚢᛁᛐᚳᛁᚾ ᛁᚾ

SNOKE
THE SUPREME LEADER

A shadowy figure at the heart of the First Order, little is known about the mysterious, wizened leader who is poised to crush the Resistance and take control of the galaxy.

Force sensitive, and highly attuned to the dark side but not a Sith, Snoke has trained Kylo Ren and at least one other apprentice.

Snoke believed General Leia Organa and Han Solo's son Ben (the grandson of Darth Vader and nephew of Jedi Master Luke Skywalker) to be adept with the dark side. He exerted his terrible influence on the young boy, corrupting him.

While his mother was aware of the influence Snoke had on Ben, she kept this from Han, believing he would not understand. Leia felt it was her role to keep Ben away from the dark side.

Eventually, Snoke turned Ben away from the light side, renaming him Kylo Ren, master of the Knights of Ren. As Ren, he carried out his master's will in destroying Luke's newly revived Jedi Order. Ren killed many of his fellow students, but Skywalker managed to escape and went into hiding. Snoke assigned Ren the job of hunting him down.

As Ren's search intensified, General Armitage Hux suggested to Snoke that he use the First Order's superweapon, Starkiller Base, to destroy the New Republic government. Agreeing to this, Snoke then ordered Ren to kill his father to overcome his temptation by the light side.

Shortly after the destruction of the Hosnian system, the center of the New Republic, Ren captured Rey—a scavenger who had seen the final piece of the map which revealed Skywalker's location—intending to use Force power to get her to reveal the location to him. Snoke was disturbed to hear that the woman resisted Ren's interrogation. Ren explained she was strong in the Force, but evidently untrained.

Snoke ordered Hux to destroy the Resistance before Skywalker could be found, and instructed Ren to bring Rey to him. But Rey managed to escape with the help of her new, burgeoning powers. As Starkiller Base was destroyed, Snoke demanded Hux escort Ren to him in order to complete his training.

Aboard the Mega-class Star Destroyer, the *Supremacy*, Snoke commands his vast army. In a show of strength and power, he addresses members of the First Order by broadcasting a towering image of himself from his throne room. Rarely appearing in public, he is protected by eight Praetorian Guards: loyal, fearsome warriors clad in red robes and armor who stand ready to defend him against attack. ●

ᛕᛕᛕᛚ ᚱᚱᛁᚤᚡᛁᚱ ᛁᚤ

KYLO REN
COMMITTED TO THE DARK SIDE

He has sacrificed everything to become the dark lord his master wishes him to be, and yet there is still conflict within Kylo Ren.

The Force is strong with Ben Solo. The son of Leia—daughter of Darth Vader and sister of Luke Skywalker—Ben trained to become a Jedi under the guidance of his uncle Luke. But the darkness swiftly rose in him, and Ben was soon seduced to the dark side by the shadowy Snoke, taking the name Kylo Ren. The malign influence of the First Order's Supreme Leader sent the young man down an ever darker path, leading him to destroy the Jedi training temple, to reject his family, and finally to murder his own father, Han Solo, on Starkiller Base.

Shortly after committing patricide, and before the mobile ice planet was destroyed, Ren faced Rey in the woods which surrounded the base. As they fought, Rey bested him, severely wounding him in single combat.

Rescued by General Hux, Kylo Ren returned to his master, to find Snoke manifestly disappointed. Snoke taunted his apprentice, further destabilizing the young man's already fractured mind. As an obedient servant, Ren follows Snoke's orders to pursue and crush the fleeing Resistance, but the words of his father echo in his mind— that Snoke is merely using him for his power.

Fueled by the dark side, Ren's ambition drives him to desire more, to plan on taking the place he thinks he deserves in the First Order. But there's something else he cannot ignore. He and the scavenger from Jakku share a strange bond in the Force, a mysterious connection whose true nature and meaning Kylo Ren is still attempting to comprehend... ●

2 /

3 /

5 /

1 / The ever-conflicted
Kylo Ren. (See
previous page)

2 / Ren surveys
the military might
of the First Order.
(See opposite page)

3 / The sinister
helmet masks the
rage beneath. (See
opposite page)

4 / Kylo Ren at his
most dangerous.

5 / Leading the attack
aboard his TIE silencer.

GENERAL HUX
THE MILITARY MASTERMIND

The brutal commander whose machinations have caused billions of deaths will not let the destruction of Starkiller Base be the end of his thirst for power.

Armitage Hux craves power above all else. The son of Imperial general Brendol Hux, Armitage didn't hesitate to eliminate his father when it became evident he represented a threat to his ascent to command.

Raised to the rank of general, Hux became the key man in Snoke's military strategy—and one of the few individuals with direct access to him. Placed in charge of Starkiller Base, the young general suggested to the Supreme Leader that they test the superweapon embedded in the ice planet and destroy the only obstacle standing in their way: the New Republic.

As he informed his troops during a passionate speech, after the disappearance of the senate, all systems would bow to the First Order. And he was correct: Even with the destruction of Starkiller Base by the Resistance, no underground movement, no planet, no system could possibly match the might of the First Order.

Moreover, Hux's engineers have developed another insidious technological breakthrough: active hyperspace tracking. With the ability to locate Resistance ships as they travel through hyperspace, Hux knows it's only a matter of time before he and the First Order can put an end to their last opponent and finally rule the galaxy.

But the obliteration of the Resistance is not Hux's only concern. Fuelled by an unquenchable thirst for power, the general surreptitiously plans his next move from the bridge of his flagship, the *Resurgent*-class Star Destroyer the *Finalizer*. And all the while he is careful to keep his thoughts hidden from both Snoke and Kylo Ren, lest his ideas of betrayal be discovered. ◉

ᒐᔦᐏᐎᐸᔑᐅᓀᐸᐎᐸᐎ ᐎᐎᕂᔑᐎᐎᓀᐎᐎᐎ ᔑᐎ

CAPTAIN PHASMA
ARMORED SYMBOL OF POWER

Taken as children from conquered worlds and trained to
serve the First Order, stormtroopers fight to restore order
and stability—and Captain Phasma is their
most feared commander.

Hailing from the harsh, primitive world of Parnassos, Phasma grew up a member of a merciless tribe whose followers were forced to kill in order to survive. When the First Order subjugated her planet, she joined its ranks to escape her savage and cruel existence.

Swearing loyalty to the First Order and its cause, Phasma developed into an unforgiving commander. She led the assault on Jakku in an attempt to retrieve the map to Luke Skywalker's location before the Resistance acquired it. When stormtrooper FN-2187 failed to carry out her orders, little did she suspect that he would go even further and desert, in the process freeing Resistance pilot Poe Dameron from prison.

Phasma and the rebellious stormtrooper crossed paths on Starkiller Base, where Finn—the traitor's new name—threatened to shoot her if she refused to take down the base shields, thus opening the way for Poe and his squadron of starfighters. Surviving the destruction of Starkiller Base, Phasma eliminated all traces of her treason, even going so far as to murder Lieutenant Sol Rivas, who could have reported her. Now Phasma waits, ready for the next opportunity to confront the anomaly FN-2187.

To accomplish that, Phasma will need to make full use of her chromium-plated armor, forged from the hull of a Naboo vessel once owned by the Emperor (and later used by General Hux's father); her combat quicksilver baton, made of a collapsible micromesh matrix, which can expand or condense at will; and her blaster rifle and customized SE-44C blaster pistol. ●

ᚹᛖᚹᛁ ᚹᛚᛟᛟᚢᚹ

STORMTROOPERS
SOLDIERS OF THE FIRST ORDER

From stormtroopers to Praetorian guards, the First Order's
army is on the rise.

STORMTROOPER

The distinctive armor of the
stormtroopers has evolved
over the years but has always
inspired fear across the galaxy.
 The men and women who
serve in the First Order have
been trained all of their lives
to bring stability by means
of strength to the galaxy in
accordance with Supreme
Leader Snoke's will.

EXECUTIONER
TROOPER

Any standard stormtrooper can
be assigned the role of executioner,
because all stormtroopers have
been trained to administer capital
punishment without hesitation.
Their laser ax brings instant justice
via its razor-sharp energy ribbons,
extended from a quartet of
collapsible claws.

Stormtroopers of the
First Order: a terrifying
symbol of power and
cruelty in the galaxy.

PRAETORIAN GUARD

THE LAST LINE OF DEFENSE

Dressed in distinctive red combat armor reminiscent of the Emperor's loyal soldiers, the Praetorian Guards stand at the ready in Snoke's throne room..

Their origins shrouded in mystery, Snoke's elite warriors seemingly possess no individual identities. Standing motionless in the throne room, they only take action when the Supreme Leader is endangered. These implacable, loyal, ever-vigilant sentinels protect Snoke from whoever may represent a threat, be it his guests, generals, or even his apprentice, Kylo Ren.

When activated, the Praetorians' layered red armor produces an intense local magnetic field that deflects blaster fire and even glancing lightsaber blows. Their tempered metal blades are made even more lethal by a high-frequency vibration created across the cutting edge by a compact ultrasonic generator. In addition, the energized blade parallel to each cutting edge can parry a lightsaber.

EIGHT COMBATANTS

There are four pairs of sentinels in the Praetorian Guard, and each pair wields the same weapons —high-tech versions of ancient analog weapons from across the galaxy: an electro-bisento, a vibro-voulge, a bilari electro-chain whip, and twin vibro-arbir blades.

CHAPTER OF OK7

FIRST
STRIKE

The First Order may have lost its most devastating weapon,
but they still have a powerful arsenal ready to strike back
against the Resistance.

AT-M6
WALKER

The All Terrain MegaCaliber
Six stands at an intimidating
36 meters tall. Its powerful
body has been built to keep
the unit stable when firing
the powerful turbolaser
cannon built into its back.

AT-ST

Taking the lead from the
Empire's All Terrain Scout
Transport, the First Order's
updated model features
improved balance, and a
stronger, less-vulnerable shell.

THE FINALIZER

The enormous command ship of General Hux is at the forefront of the siege of D'Qar.

TIE SILENCER

A prototype ship, this formidable craft is piloted by Kylo Ren as he leads Special Forces in their attack on the *Raddus*.

TIE/SF FIGHTER

Despite being fast and maneuverable, the TIE fighter defence of the Starkiller Base was found wanting, leaving the surviving pilots with a lot to prove.

UPSILON COMMAND SHUTTLE

An imposing craft, used by high-ranking First Order officers, including Kylo Ren.

DJ
SHOW HIM THE MONEY

Con artists can be found in any prison in the galaxy, and they all have something in common: It's best not to trust them!

The assorted thieves and pickpockets who wind up in the Canto Bight jail ordinarily don't plan on getting caught...all except for one. Unlikely as it seems, DJ actually lets the local police arrest him on purpose; for as he explains to all his cellmates, jail is the only place where he can sleep without worrying about the authorities.

A cynical survivor and a self-proclaimed victim of societal inequity, DJ only cares about one thing: money. Such is his mercenary nature that he would happily work for the Resistance or the First Order, his choice determined by how much money he would make out of the deal.

That kind of attitude perfectly reflects his only belief, as well as his nickname: Don't Join. To DJ, following a greater cause like the Resistance or the First Order is a game. Sooner or later, followers of either end up dead—and DJ will do anything he can to survive.

While he's been accused of many things, being a bad codebreaker is not one of them. With his modified Zinbiddle card, DJ can crack open the cell doors of the Canto Bight jail at any time he feels, while his specially handcrafted keys can temporarily bypass even bio-hexacrypt-protected data networks. ☻

CANTO BIGHT

WHERE THE WEALTHY RULE

On a planet far from the chaos, conflict, and suffering they helped cause, war profiteers reap the benefits of their amoral ways.

1 /

There's no place in the galaxy quite like the resort city of Canto Bight on planet Cantonica—a haven for those shady individuals making their fortunes by entering into contracts with the First Order, supplying its armories, or selling weapons, ammunition, and technology to independent groups preparing for a galactic war. In Canto Bight, local law enforcement is in the palm of the hand of the city's wealthy denizens, constantly patrolling the resort's streets, artificial coastline, and the Canto Casino and Racetrack.

This celebrated exclusive club—which boasts luxurious restaurants, a deluxe hotel, a shopping concourse, game rooms, and a fathiers racetrack— is where the galaxy's elite spends its wealth, taking chances at games like Savareen Whist, Zinbiddle, Uvide, and Hazard Toss (the clientele's favorite dice game). Only politicians, celebrities, and business magnates can afford these expensive pleasures—but spies and master codebreakers can hide themselves among them...

1 / Thamm, the best croupier in the business!

2 / Snook Uccorfay with Derla Pidys. (See opposite page)

3 / Assorted gamblers try their luck at the casino's tables.

4 / Performance artists Rhomby and Parallela Grammus.

5 / The mysterious, alluring "Lovey."

6 / The Contessa Alissyndrex delga Cantonica Provincion.

3 /

4 /

5 /

6 /

7 / Neepers
Panpick

ꞓꝨꞓꞀꞀꞐꝨ ꝆꞓꝨꞀ ꝌꞩꝆꞐꝌꞐꝆ

RIAN JOHNSON
DIRECTOR ON SET

Go behind-the-scenes to see *Star Wars: The Last Jedi*'s visonary
director Rian Johnson at work, and sometimes play...

2 /

1 / Offering some direction to Joonas Suotamo (Chewbacca). (See opposite page)

2 / Sharing a joke with John Boyega (Finn) and Oscar Isaac (Poe Dameron).

3 / A moment's contemplation with Carrie Fisher (General Organa).

4 / Lining up a shot with a tough-looking Daisy Ridley (Rey).

3 /

4 /

5 /

5 / Taking a break on the island of Skellig Michael, which doubles as Ahch-To.

6 / Johnson flanked by producers Ram Bergman and Kathleen Kennedy.

7 / Johnson and Bergman share a moment with Joonas Suotamo (Chewbacca). (See opposite page)

8 / The things we do for *Star Wars*! Johnson and the crew shoot on a waterlogged set. (See opposite page)

6 /

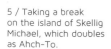

8 /

9 /

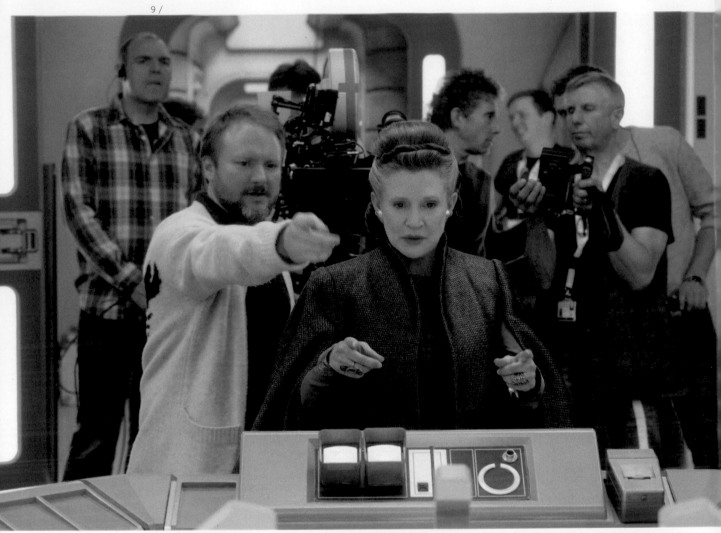

10 /

9 / Directing Carrie Fisher as Leia takes command of the *Raddus*.

10 / Bergman and Johnson relax on a Resistance transport.

11 / Johnson cheekily signs the *Millennium Falcon,* replacing the former and future *Star Wars* director JJ Abrams! (See opposite page)

12 / Photoreceptor level with BB-8. Jimmy Vee, the actor who plays R2-D2 in *The Last Jedi,* can been seen to the left of this shot. (See opposite page)

11 /

12 /

↓ΞⱯⅠ Ɫⵌↆ ◁Ⴑ ▢Ⱪⵌ

ART
FROM A THOUSAND WORLDS
Presenting a gallery of stunning concept art.

1 / The last line of defense. The Resistance take to the trenches on Crait. Art by Kevin Jenkins.

2 /

2 / The First Order scores a direct hit on the hangar bay as Poe and BB-8 are knocked back! Art by Kevin Jenkins.

3 /

4 /

5 /

3 / Luke, Chewie, and Rey keep warm on a cold Ahch-To night. Art by James Carson and Rick Heinrichs

4 / The well-to-do visitors to Canto Bight mingle. Art by Mauro Borelli and Aaron McBride

5 / Luke looks on as Rey meditates. Art by Justin Sweet.

6 / No friend of BB-8: Meet BB-9E! Art by Jake Lunt Davies. (See opposite page)

OTHER GREAT TIE-IN COMPANIONS FROM TITAN
ON SALE NOW!

Rogue One - The Official Collector's Edition
ISBN 9781785861574

Rogue One - The Official Mission Debrief
ISBN 9781785861581

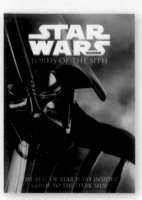

Star Wars: Lords of the Sith
ISBN 9781785851919

Star Wars: Heroes of the Force
ISBN 9781785851926

Star Wars: Icons Of The Galaxy
ISBN 9781785851933

The Best of Star Wars Insider Volume 1
ISBN 9781785851162

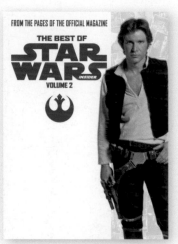

The Best of Star Wars Insider Volume 2
ISBN 9781785851179

The Best of Star Wars Insider Volume 3
ISBN 9781785851896

The Best of Star Wars Insider Volume 4
ISBN 9781785851902

Star Trek: The Movies
ISBN 9781785855924

Fifty Years of Star Trek
ISBN 9781785855931

Star Trek - A Next Generation Companion
ISBN 9781785855948

Star Trek Beyond Collector's Edition
ISBN 9781785860096

Star Trek Discovery Collector's Edition
ISBN 9781785861581

TITANCOMICS
For more information visit www.titan-comics.com